THE ADVENTURES OF
KING
ARTHUR

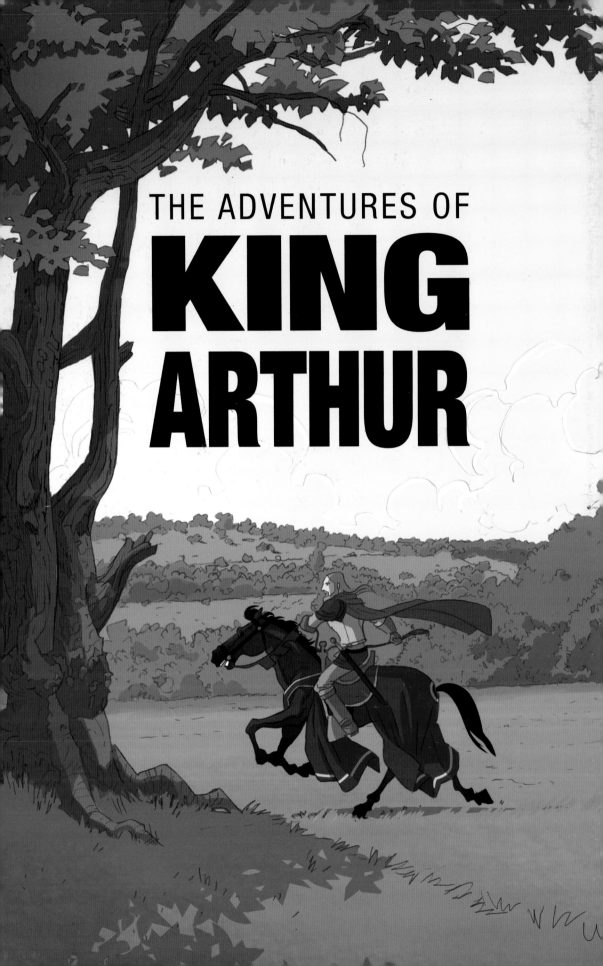

THE ADVENTURES OF
KING
ARTHUR

Retold by Russell Punter

Illustrated by Andrea da Rold

Series editors: Lesley Sims & Jane Chisholm

Consultant: Mike Collins

The World of King Arthur

Tintagel Castle

Tintagel •

The site of Arthur's final battle

CORNWALL

ENGLISH

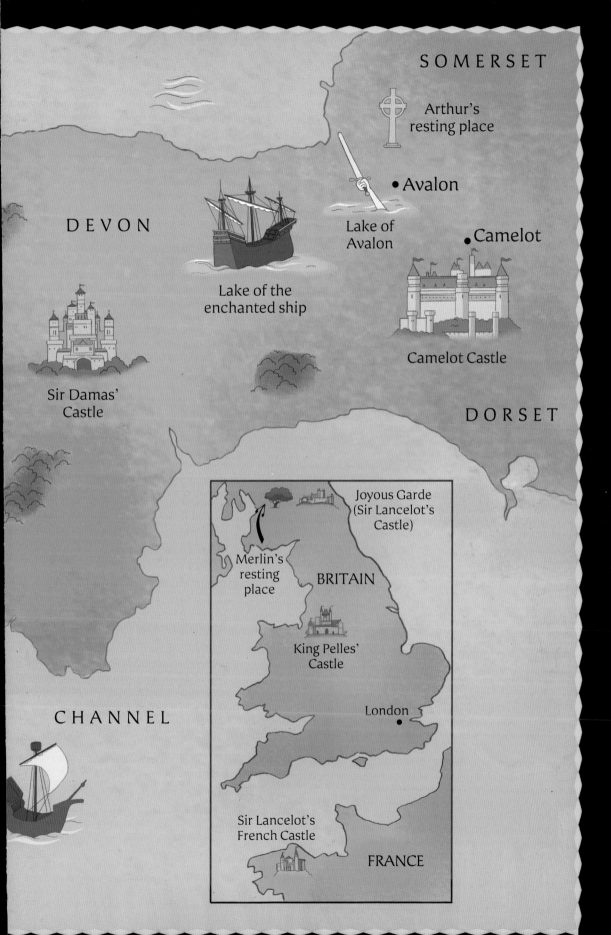

Many years ago, Britain was a thrilling land of brave knights and magnificent castles, ruled by the bold King Uther Pendragon.

While he lived, the kingdom was a safe and peaceful place. But one wise man had seen a dark and terrible future. Even now, that man was on his way to Tintagel Castle to warn the king...

THE WISE WIZARD'S PREDICTION COMES TRUE – THE KING SOON FALLS ILL AND DIES, AND A VIOLENT SERIES OF BRUTAL BATTLES BEGINS FOR THE CROWN...

THE KINGDOM IS THROWN INTO CHAOS...

MUCH BLOOD IS SPILLED...

BUT NO ONE EMERGES TO UNITE THE LAND.

SIXTEEN YEARS LATER, MERLIN VISITS THE ARCHBISHOP IN LONDON...

THESE ARE **DARK DAYS**, MERLIN.

NOT FOR MUCH LONGER, MY FRIEND...

I WANT YOU TO GATHER THE LAND'S **MOST NOBLE KNIGHTS** HERE, ON CHRISTMAS DAY.

KNIGHT AFTER KNIGHT TRIES TO REMOVE THE SWORD, WITHOUT SUCCESS...

IT'S A **TRICK**!

IT MUST BE **STUCK**!

NO MAN COULD SHIFT IT!

AND SO, THE BISHOP ISSUES AN INVITATION TO EVERY KNIGHT IN THE KINGDOM...

A FEW DAYS LATER, AT THE HOUSE OF SIR ECTOR AND HIS SONS, SIR KAY AND ARTHUR...

GRAND TOURNAMENT

London
New Year's Day

To conclude with a contest to remove the famous sword from the stone.

WHAT ARE YOU **DOING**, KAY?

PREPARING FOR A **TOURNAMENT** IN LONDON.

YOU CAN BE HIS **SQUIRE**, ARTHUR.

EARLY ON NEW YEAR'S DAY, ECTOR AND HIS SONS ARRIVE IN LONDON FOR THE TOURNAMENT. AFTER TAKING LODGINGS AT A NEARBY INN...

KAY! THE TOURNAMENT IS ABOUT TO **BEGIN.**

I DON'T BELIEVE IT! I MUST HAVE LEFT MY **SWORD** AT THE INN.

I'LL RUN BACK AND GET IT FOR YOU.

BUT WHEN ARTHUR REACHES THE INN...

THE PLACE IS **LOCKED!**

EVERYONE MUST BE AT THE TOURNAMENT.

ARTHUR IS RACING BACK, WHEN...

A SWORD!

ARTHUR AND MERLIN RETURN TO CAMELOT...

YOU WERE **RIGHT**, MERLIN. THIS IS THE **FINEST** SWORD I'VE **EVER** SEEN!

TRUE, SIRE. BUT THE **SCABBARD** IS **MORE** POWERFUL.

WHILE YOU WEAR IT, YOU'LL **NEVER** SHED A DROP OF BLOOD IN BATTLE.

LANCELOT TELLS THE COURT ABOUT MERLIN'S LAST REQUEST...

WELL IF MERLIN WISHED YOU TO BE A KNIGHT, THEN I **MUST** COMPLY...

KNEEL!

ARISE, SIR LANCELOT!

NIMUE LEADS THE NEW KNIGHT TO THE WOUNDED MAN, AND...

HE'S DONE IT!

WHILE LANCELOT STRUGGLES WITH HIS CONSCIENCE, SOME AT CAMELOT HAVE ACTUALLY TURNED AGAINST ARTHUR...

THE KING'S HALF-SISTER, MORGAN LE FAY, HAS MYSTICAL POWERS. NOW SHE PLANS TO USE THEM AGAINST HER BROTHER, WITH THE HELP OF SIR ACCOLON...

OUR MEETING MUST BE **QUICK**. ARTHUR **KNOWS** OF MY POWERS AND IS **SUSPICIOUS** ABOUT MY **AMBITIONS**. WE MAY BE DISCOVERED AT **ANY MOMENT**.

SOON I WILL ASK YOU TO **FIGHT** FOR ME, ACCOLON. WILL YOU DO THAT?

TO THE **DEATH!** I'D SLAY **ANYONE** FOR YOUR LOVE.

EVEN THE KING HIMSELF?

IF YOU **WISHED** IT...

THANK YOU, MY LOVE. NOW **GO**, AND AWAIT MY **COMMAND**.

45

ACCOLON'S SWORD FALLS FROM HIS GRASP...

...TO BE RETRIEVED BY ARTHUR..

IT'S **EXCALIBUR!** I CAN FEEL IT!

ARTHUR GRABS HIS OPPONENT'S SCABBARD...

WHEN ARTHUR WAKES IN THE NIGHT...

ARTHUR RUNS TO THE ABBESS...

WHO CAME WHILE I SLEPT?

ONLY YOUR SISTER, SIRE. SHE SAID...

THE SCABBARD!?

ARTHUR SUMMONS HIS KNIGHTS AND RIDES IN PURSUIT OF MORGAN...

AS DAWN BREAKS...

YES SIRE. A LADY AND MANY MEN. THEY HEADED TOWARDS THE FOREST.

HAS ANYONE PASSED THIS WAY, FELLOW?

SPLASH!

MORGAN RIDES ON, DESPERATELY, OUT OF THE FOREST...

...AND INTO A STONY VALLEY...

ONE YEAR LATER, ARTHUR AND HIS KNIGHTS ARE FEASTING AT THE ROUND TABLE. BUT AS USUAL, ONE CHAIR REMAINS EMPTY – THE SO-CALLED 'PERILOUS SEAT'...

...THIS SEAT IS RESERVED FOR THE FINEST KNIGHT IN THE WORLD. IT'S SAID THAT ANY OTHER KNIGHT WHO SITS THERE WILL DIE.

SUDDENLY, SUPERNATURAL LETTERS OF FIRE APPEAR ON THE CHAIR...

A knight destined for greatness shall come to this chair...

A knight destined for greatness shall come to this chair...

THE SEAT TRULY IS **ENCHANTED**!

MOMENTS LATER...

GREETINGS, YOUR MAJESTY. MY NAME IS **NACIENS**.

THIS IS MY WARD, **GALAHAD**. HE'S COME TO TAKE HIS PLACE AT THE ROUND TABLE.

IS HE A **KNIGHT**?

NOT YET. BUT IT IS HIS **DESTINY**. BEHOLD...

This is the seat of Sir Galahad, the world's best knight.

IT **MUST** BE SO!

KNIGHT THIS BOY, LANCELOT. FOR HE'LL SURELY BE THE **GREATEST** OF US ALL.

AND SO...

ARISE, SIR GALAHAD!

THE NEW KNIGHT WALKS TO THE PERILOUS SEAT...

AND CALMLY SITS...

LET US **DRINK** TO SIR GALAHAD!

SIR GALAHAD!

KILL THE STRANGER!

CHARGE!

SIR PERCIVAL MUST FIGHT FOR HIS LIFE...

AGGH!

THEN HIS HORSE IS FELLED BENEATH HIM...

NEEEIGH!

PERCIVAL IS READY TO FIGHT BACK...

YOU FIENDS!

FAREWELL GALAHAD.

PERCIVAL RETURNS TO CAMELOT AND TELLS THE COURT WHAT HAS HAPPENED...

IT SEEMS SIR GALAHAD TRULY **WAS** THE **GREATEST KNIGHT.**

THE QUEST IS **OVER,** YOUR MAJESTY.

MORDRED TELLS ARTHUR WHAT AGRAVAIN HAS SEEN...

I DON'T BELIEVE IT!

SIR AGRAVAIN IS LOYAL TO YOU, AS AM I. HE WOULD NOT LIE....

ENOUGH! I WILL HEAR NO MORE!

THE BLIND FOOL! I MUST GET PROOF HE CAN'T DENY.

THE NEXT EVENING, LANCELOT VISITS THE QUEEN IN HER CHAMBER...

...UNAWARE THAT MORDRED'S SPIES ARE WATCHING.

HOW CAN WE GO ON MEETING LIKE THIS? I HAVE NO WISH TO HURT THE KING.

NOR I...

THUMP!

THUMP!

TRAITOR KNIGHT! COME OUT, NOW, YOU'RE SURROUNDED!

SOON MORDRED IS THE ONLY SURVIVOR. BADLY WOUNDED, HE HAS NO CHOICE BUT TO FLEE...

THE KING WILL WANT US **BOTH** DEAD NOW. **RUN AWAY WITH ME!**

I **CAN'T!** GO, LANCELOT, BUT DON'T FORGET ME.

WHILE LANCELOT ESCAPES, MORDRED TELLS THE KING WHAT HAS HAPPENED...

THEN THE FELLOWSHIP OF THE ROUND TABLE IS **BROKEN!**

YET LANCELOT WAS A **POPULAR** MAN. MANY KNIGHTS ARE SURE TO SIDE WITH HIM.

AND WHAT OF THE **QUEEN?** TREASON IS PUNISHABLE BY **DEATH,** YOUR MAJESTY.

I KNOW THAT **ONLY TOO WELL.**

RAAA!

URRGH!

AGH!

AGGH!

THE FIGHT IS LONG AND FIERCE. THEN, IN AN UNGUARDED MOMENT, ARTHUR IS KNOCKED FROM HIS HORSE...

AGGH!

SHALL I **KILL** HIM, LANCELOT?

NO, SIR BORS! THERE HAS BEEN **ENOUGH** BLOOD SPILLED.

I **NEVER** HAD ANY DESIRE TO FIGHT MY **FRIEND** AND **KING.** LET US CALL A **TRUCE** NOW.

I LOVE GUINEVERE, BUT SHE IS YOUR **QUEEN.** I HAVE **WRONGED** YOU. **PLEASE** TAKE HER BACK. I SHALL LEAVE THE KINGDOM **FOREVER.**

THERE ARE **FEW** MEN I COULD **ALLOW** TO LIVE AFTER WHAT YOU'VE DONE. BUT I BELIEVE YOU TO BE **TRULY** SORRY.

LANCELOT TAKES ARTHUR INTO HIS CASTLE...

HERE IS YOUR QUEEN. SHE HAS BEEN **TRUE** TO YOU, I **SWEAR** IT.

THOSE WHO SAY OTHERWISE ONLY WISH TO **DESTROY** THE FELLOWSHIP OF THE ROUND TABLE.

A FINAL, BRUTAL BATTLE ENSUES...

SOON ONE HUNDRED THOUSAND KNIGHTS LIE DEAD.

HIS MIND FULL OF SADNESS, BEDEVERE SPENDS THE NIGHT WANDERING THE COUNTRYSIDE...

AT SUNRISE, HE FINDS HIMSELF AT A HALF-HIDDEN CHAPEL...

THAT GRAVE LOOKS **FRESHLY DUG.**

WHO'S **BURIED HERE,** FATHER?

I DON'T KNOW HIS NAME.

LAST NIGHT SOME LADIES BROUGHT HIS BODY HERE AND ASKED ME TO BURY HIM.

THIS MUST BE **ARTHUR'S** GRAVE!

I SHALL **NEVER** LEAVE HIS SIDE.

SHORTLY AFTERWARDS, ARTHUR'S BELOVED GUINEVERE LEAVES THIS WORLD AND IS PLACED ALONGSIDE HER KING BY THE FAITHFUL LANCELOT.

SOON, BOTH HE AND BEDEVERE, THE LAST OF THE KNIGHTS OF THE ROUND TABLE, ARE NO MORE.

SOME SAY THAT ONE DAY, WHEN ARTHUR'S KINGDOM NEEDS HIM, HE WILL RETURN.

UNTIL THAT TIME, HE SLEEPS...

...IN A HIDDEN CORNER OF A FORGOTTEN FOREST...

...WHERE HIS TOMBSTONE TELLS OF A LEGENDARY RULER, WAITING TO LIVE ONCE MORE...

HERE LIES ARTHUR,
THE ONCE
AND
FUTURE KING

THE END

The Legend of King Arthur

Tales of King Arthur and his knights have been told for hundreds of years. But are they merely stories, or was Arthur a real ruler of Ancient Britain?

Some of the earliest known mentions of Arthur come from Welsh and Breton stories and poems of the 5th and 6th centuries.

Arthur's role in these tales varies. In some, his enemies are Saxon invaders. In others they are dragons, giants and witches. Certain poems link Arthur with Annwn, the Welsh Otherworld, a place separate from everyday reality. Arthur is also mentioned in Welsh Triads, which were written descriptions of Welsh folklore, mythology and traditional history.

Probably the most significant account of Arthur's life and times came in *Historia Regum Britanniae* (*History of the Kings of Britain*). This was a semi-historical account of British history up to the 7th century, written around 1136 by Geoffrey of Monmouth.

Geoffrey's retelling portrays Arthur as the King of Britain who defeats Saxon invaders before building an empire. The tale mentions Uther Pendragon, Arthur's father, as well as many of the other figures associated with the legend, such as Merlin, Guinevere, Kay, Bedevere and Mordred, along with the sword Excalibur.

A French writer named Chrétien de Troyes wrote five Arthurian romances between 1170 and 1190. These introduced Lancelot and the Holy Grail to the story, together with a passing reference to Camelot, the castle at the heart of Arthur's kingdom.

The first half of the 13th century saw the Vulgate Cycle of stories: five French works which introduced the character of Galahad, developed Merlin's role and established Camelot as King Arthur's court.

In the late 15th century, English writer Thomas Malory retold the whole legend in *Le Morte d'Arthur*. Malory based his story on the previous romances, in particular the Vulgate Cycle. When it was published in 1485, *Le Morte d'Arthur* was one of the earliest printed books in England.

After the end of the Middle Ages, the Arthurian legend fell out of popularity. When it did make an appearance – as in *The History of Tom Thumb* – it tended to be treated less seriously. Published in 1621, *Tom Thumb* was the first fairy tale to be printed in English and it featured the tiny hero entertaining King Arthur's court.

In *The Lady of Shalott*, the heroine travels to Camelot, but dies before she can enter the castle.

The 19th century, however, brought a revival in interest in the legend. *Le Morte d'Arthur* was published in 1816 for the first time since 1634.

Alfred Lord Tennyson, Poet Laureate of Great Britain and Ireland, wrote several Arthurian poems including *The Lady of Shalott*, first published in 1832, and *Sir Lancelot and Queen Guinevere*, published ten years later. He went on to write *Idylls of the King*, published between 1859 and 1885, a series of twelve poems which covered Arthur's entire life.

Arthurian legend inspired other poets and writers, such as William Wordsworth (1770-1850) and William Morris (1834-1896), as well as artists such as Edward Burne-Jones who painted *The Last Sleep of Arthur in Avalon* between 1881 and 1898. In America, author Sidney Lanier wrote *The Boy's King Arthur* (1880) and the legend became the inspiration for Mark Twain's *A Connecticut Yankee in King Arthur's Court* (1889).

Later retellings included T.H. White's *The Once and Future King* (1958), which was loosely taken from *Le Morte d'Arthur* and was adapted into a stage musical, *Camelot* (1960), and a Disney animated feature film, *The Sword in the Stone* (1963).

Other film versions of the legend include *Camelot* (1967), *First Knight* (1995) and *King Arthur* (2004).

There have also been numerous television adaptations over the years, including *The Adventures of Sir Lancelot* (1956–57), *Arthur of the Britons* (1972–1973), *The Legend of King Arthur* (1979), *Merlin* (2008–2012) and *Camelot* (2011).

So did King Arthur really exist? Some people believe so. *The Historia Brittonum*, a history of Britain written around the year 828, lists twelve battles fought by Arthur. But it doesn't refer to him as a king and some historians have questioned its reliability.

Arthurian characters are also referred to in the *Annales Cambriae*, a chronicle of British history compiled from the 10th to 13th centuries, but many other contemporary histories make no mention of Arthur at all.

It's thought by some that Glastonbury in the county of Somerset is the site of the Isle of Avalon. Among the ruins of Glastonbury Abbey are tombstones which claim to mark the final resting place of Arthur and Guinevere.

However, most historians think it unlikely that the King Arthur of legend really existed, or argue at least that real evidence has yet to emerge.

Russell Punter was born in Bedfordshire, England. From an early age he enjoyed writing and illustrating his own stories. He trained as a graphic designer at art college in West Sussex before entering publishing in 1987. He has written over fifty books for children, ranging from original rhyming stories to adaptations of classic novels.

Andrea da Rold was born in Milan, Italy. He graduated from Milan's prestigious Academy of Fine Arts, and he still lives in the city today. He works as a cartoonist for Star Comics (*Samuel Sand, Lazarus Ledd*) and as an illustrator of children's books, working with, among others, Mondadori, De Agostini and Giunti. He illustrates the covers of the very popular *Geronimo Stilton* for Piemme and collaborates on Mondadori's *Focus Jr.* magazine.

Mike Collins has been creating comics for over 25 years. Starting on *Spider-Man* and *Transformers* for Marvel UK, he has also worked for DC, 2000AD and a host of other publishers. In that time he's written or drawn almost all the major characters for each company – *Wonder Woman, Batman, Superman, Flash, Teen Titans, X-Men, Captain Britain, Judge Dredd, Sláine, Rogue Trooper, Darkstars, Peter Cannon: Thunderbolt* and more. He currently draws a series of noir crime fiction graphic novels, *Varg Veum.* He also provides storyboards for TV and films, including *Doctor Who, Sherlock, Igam Ogam, Claude, Hana's Helpline* and *Horrid Henry.*

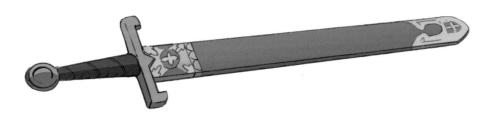

Cover design: Matt Preston

First published in 2017 by Usborne Publishing Ltd., Usborne House, 83-85 Saffron Hill, London EC1N 8RT, England. www.usborne.com
Copyright © 2017 Usborne Publishing Ltd.